# *Jacob Behmen*

*Alexander Whyte*

# JACOB BEHMEN

BY
Alexander Whyte

# Jacob Behmen

Jacob Behmen, the greatest of the mystics, and the father of German philosophy, was all his life nothing better than a working shoemaker. He was born at Old Seidenberg, a village near Goerlitz in Silesia, in the year 1575, and he died at Goerlitz in the year 1624. Jacob Behmen has no biography. Jacob Behmen's books are his best biography. While working with his hands, Jacob Behmen's whole life was spent in the deepest and the most original thought; in piercing visions of GOD and of nature; in prayer, in praise, and in love to GOD and man. Of Jacob Behmen it may be said with the utmost truth and soberness that he lived and moved and had his being in GOD. Jacob Behmen has no biography because his whole life was hid with CHRIST in GOD.

\* \* \* \* \*

While we have nothing that can properly be called a biography of Jacob Behmen, we have ample amends made to us in those priceless morsels of autobiography that lie scattered so plentifully up and down all his books. And nothing could be more charming than just those incidental and unstudied utterances of Behmen about himself. Into the very depths of a passage of the profoundest speculation Behmen will all of a sudden throw a few verses of the most childlike and heart-winning confidences about his own mental history and his own spiritual experience. And thus it is that, without at all intending it, Behmen has left behind him a complete history of his great mind and his holy heart in those outbursts of diffidence, deprecation, explanation, and self-defence, of which his philosophical and theological, as well as his apologetic and experimental, books are all so full. It were an immense service done to our best literature if some of Behmen's students would go through all Behmen's books, so as to make a complete collection and composition of the best of those autobiographic passages. Such a book, if it were well done, would at once take rank with |*The Confessions*| of ST. AUGUSTINE, |*The Divine Comedy*| of DANTE, and the |*Grace Abounding*| of JOHN BUNYAN. It would then be seen by all, what few, till then, will believe, that Jacob Behmen's mind and heart and spiritual experience all combine to give him a foremost place among the most classical masters in that great field.

In the nineteenth chapter of the |*Aurora*| there occurs a very important passage of this autobiographic nature. In that famous passage Behmen tells his readers that when his eyes first began to be opened, the sight of this world completely overwhelmed him. ASAPH'S experiences, so powerfully set before us in the seventy-third Psalm, will best convey, to those who do not know Behmen, what Behmen also passed through before he drew near to GOD. Like that so thoughtful Psalmist, Behmen's steps had well-nigh slipped when he saw the prosperity of the wicked, and when he saw how waters of a full cup were so often wrung out to the people of GOD. The mystery of life, the sin and misery of life, cast Behmen into a deep and inconsolable melancholy. No Scripture could comfort him. His thoughts of GOD were such that he will not allow himself, even after they are long past, to put them down on paper. In this terrible trouble he lifted up his heart to GOD, little knowing, as yet, what GOD was, or what his own heart was. Only, he wrapped up his whole heart, and mind, and will, and desire in the love and the mercy of GOD: determined not to give over till GOD had heard him and had helped him. 'And then, when I had wholly hazarded my life upon what I was doing, my whole spirit seemed to me suddenly to break through the gates of hell, and to be taken up into the arms and the heart of GOD. I can compare it to nothing else but the resurrection at the last day. For then, with all reverence I say it, with the eyes of my spirit I saw GOD. I saw both what GOD is, and I saw how GOD is what He is. And with that there came a mighty and an incontrollable impulse to set it down, so as to preserve what I had seen. Some men will mock me, and will tell me to stick to my proper trade, and not trouble my mind with philosophy and theology. Let these high matters alone. Leave them to those who have both the time and the talent for them, they will say. So I have often said to myself, but the truth of GOD did burn in my bones till I took pen and ink and began to set down what I had seen. All this time do not mistake me for a saint or an angel. My heart also is full of all evil. In malice, and in hatred, and in lack of brotherly love, after all I have seen and experienced, I am like all other men. I am surely the fullest of all men of all manner of infirmity and malignity.' Behmen protests in every book of his that what he has written he has received immediately from GOD. 'Let it never be imagined that I am any greater or any better than other men. When the Spirit of GOD is taken away from me I cannot even read so as to understand what I have myself written. I have every day to wrestle with the devil and with my own heart, no man in all the world more. Oh no! thou must not for one moment think of me as if I had by my own power or holiness climbed up into heaven or descended into the abyss. Oh no! hear me. I am as thou art. I have no more light than thou hast. Let no man think of me what I am not. But what I am all men may be who will truly believe, and will truly wrestle for truth and goodness under JESUS CHRIST. I marvel every day that GOD should reveal both the Divine Nature and Temporal and Eternal Nature for the first time to such a simple and unlearned man as I am. But what am I to resist what GOD will do? What am I to say but, Behold the son of thine handmaiden! I have often besought Him to take these too high and too deep matters away from off me, and to commit them to men of more learning and of a better style of speech. But He always put my prayer away from Him and continued to kindle His fire in my bones. And with all my striving to quench GOD'S spirit of revelation, I found that I had only by that gathered the more stones for the house that He had ordained me to build for Him and for His children in this world.'

Jacob Behmen's first book, his |*Aurora*|, was not a book at all, but a bundle of loose leaves. Nothing was further from Behmen's mind, when he took up his pen of an evening, than to make a book. He took up his pen after his day's work was over in order to preserve for his own memory and use in after days the revelations that had been made to him, and the experiences and exercises through which GOD had passed him. And, besides, Jacob Behmen could not have written a book even if he had tried it. He was a total stranger to the world of books; and then, over and above that, he had been taken up into a world of things into which no book ever written as yet had dared to enter. Again, and again, and again, till it came to fill his whole life, Behmen would be sitting over his work, or walking abroad under the stars, or worshipping in his pew in the parish church, when, like the captive prophet by the river of Chebar, he would be caught up by the hair of the head and carried away into the visions of GOD to behold the glory of GOD. And then, when he came to himself, there would arise within him a 'fiery instigation' to set down for a 'memorial' what he had again seen and heard. 'The gate of the Divine Mystery was sometimes so opened to me that in one quarter of an hour I saw and knew more than if I had been many years together at a university. At which I did exceedingly admire, and, though it passed my understanding how it happened, I thereupon turned my heart to GOD to praise Him for it. For I saw and knew the Being of all Beings; the Byss and the Abyss; as, also, the Generation of the Son and the Procession of the Spirit. I saw the descent and original of this world also, and of all its creatures. I saw in their order and outcome the Divine world, the angelical world, paradise, and then this fallen and dark world of our own. I saw the beginning of the good and the evil, and the true origin and existence of each of them. All of which did not only cause me great wonder but also a great joy and a great fear. And then it came with commanding power into my mind that I must set down the same in pen and ink for a memorial to myself; albeit, I could hardly contain or express what I had seen. For twelve years this went on in me. Sometimes the truth would hit me like a sudden smiting storm of rain; and then there would be the clear sunshine after the rain. All which was to teach me that GOD will manifest Himself in the soul of man after what manner and what measure it pleases Him and as it seems good in His sight.'

No human being knew all this time what Jacob Behmen was passing through, and he never intended that any human being should know. But, with all his humility, and all his love of obscurity, he could not remain hidden. Just how it came about we are not fully told; but, long before his book was finished, a nobleman in the neighbourhood, who was deeply interested in the philosophy and the theology of that day, somehow got hold of Behmen's papers and had them copied out and spread abroad, to Behmen's great surprise and great distress. Copy after copy was stealthily made of Behmen's manuscript, till, most unfortunately for both of them, a copy came into the hands of Behmen's parish minister. But for that accident, so to call it, we would never have heard the name of GREGORY RICHTER, First Minister of Goerlitz, nor could we have believed that any minister of JESUS CHRIST could have gone so absolutely mad with ignorance and envy and anger and ill-will. The libel is still preserved that Behmen's minister drew out against the author of |*Aurora*|, and the only thing it proves to us is this, that its author must have been a dull-headed, coarse-hearted, foul-mouthed man. Richter's persecution of poor Behmen caused Behmen lifelong trouble; but, at the same time, it served to advertise his genius to his generation, and to manifest to all men the meekness, the humility, the docility, and the love of peace of the persecuted man. 'Pastor-Primarius Richter,' says a bishop of his own communion, 'was a man full of hierarchical arrogance and pride. He had only the most outward apprehension of the dogmatics of his day, and he was totally incapable of understanding Jacob Behmen.' But it is not for the limitations of his understanding that Pastor Richter stands before us so laden with blame. The school is a small one still that, after two centuries of study and prayer and a holy life, can pretend to understand the whole of the |*Aurora*|. WILLIAM LAW, a man of the best understanding, and of the humblest heart, tells us that his first reading of Behmen put him into a 'perfect sweat' of astonishment and awe. No wonder, then, that a man of Gregory Richter's narrow mind and hard heart was thrown into such a sweat of prejudice and anger and ill will.

I do not propose to take you down into the deep places where Jacob Behmen dwells and works. And that for a very good reason. For I have found no firm footing in those deep places for my own feet. I wade in and in to the utmost of my ability, and still there rise up above me, and stretch out around me, and sink down beneath me, vast reaches of revelation and speculation, attainment and experience, before which I can only wonder and worship. See Jacob Behmen working with his hands in his solitary stall, when he is suddenly caught up into heaven till he beholds in enraptured vision The Most High Himself. And then, after that, see him swept down to hell, down to sin, and down into the bottomless pit of the human heart. Jacob Behmen, almost more than any other man whatsoever, is carried up till he moves like a holy angel or a glorified saint among things unseen and eternal. Jacob Behmen is of the race of the seers, and he stands out a very prince among them. He is full of eyes, and all his eyes are full of light. It does not stagger me to hear his disciples calling him, as HEGEL does, 'a man of a mighty mind,' or, as LAW does, 'the illuminated Behmen,' and 'the blessed Behmen.' 'In speculative power,' says dry DR. KURTZ, 'and in poetic wealth, exhibited with epic and dramatic effect, Behmen's system surpasses everything of the kind ever written.' Some of his disciples have the hardihood to affirm indeed that even ISAAC NEWTON ploughed with Behmen's heifer, but had not the boldness to acknowledge the debt. I entirely accept it when his disciples assert it of their master that he had a privilege and a passport permitted him such as no mortal man has had the like since JOHN'S eyes closed upon his completed Apocalypse. After repeated and prolonged reading of Behmen's amazing books, nothing that has been said by his most ecstatic disciples about their adored master either astonishes or offends me. Dante himself does not beat such a soaring wing as Behmen's; and all the trumpets that sound in |*Paradise Lost*| do not swell my heart and chase its blood like Jacob Behmen's broken syllables about the Fall. I would not wonder to have it pointed out to me in the world to come that all that Gichtel, and St. Martin, and Hegel, and Law, and Walton, and Martensen, and Hartmann have said about Jacob Behmen and his visions of GOD and Nature and Man were all but literally true. No doubt,--nay, the thing is certain,--that if you open Jacob Behmen anywhere as Gregory Richter opened the |*Aurora*|; if a new idea is a pain and a provocation to you; if you have any prejudice in your heart for any reason against Behmen; if you dislike the sound of his name because some one you dislike has discovered him and praised him, or because you do not yourself already know him and love him, then, no doubt, you will find plenty in Behmen at which to stumble, and which will amply justify you in anything you wish to say against him. But if you are a true student and a good man; if you are an open-minded and a humble-minded man; if you are prepared to sit at any man's feet who will engage to lead you a single step out of your ignorance and your evil; if you open Behmen with a predisposition to believe in him, and with the expectation and the determination to get good out of him,--then, in the measure of all that; in the measure of your capacity of mind and your hospitality of heart; in the measure of your humility, seriousness, patience, teachableness, hunger for truth, hunger for righteousness,--in that measure you will find Jacob Behmen to be what MAURICE tells us he found him to be, 'a generative thinker.' Out of much you cannot understand,--wherever the blame for that may lie,--out of much slag and much dross, I am mistaken if you will not lay up some of your finest gold; and out of much straw and chaff some of the finest of the wheat. The Divine Nature, human nature, time, space, matter, life, love, sin, death, holiness, heaven, hell,--Behmen's reader must have lived and moved all his days among such things as these: he must be at home, as far as the mind of man can be at home, among such things as these, and then he will begin to understand Behmen, and will still strive better and better to understand him; and, where he does not as yet understand him, he will set that down to his own inattention, incapacity, want of due preparation, and want of the proper ripeness for such a study.

At the same time let all intending students of Jacob Behmen take warning that they will have to learn an absolutely new and an unheard-of language if they would speak with Behmen and have Behmen speak with them.  For Behmen's books are written neither in German nor in English of any age or idiom, but in the most original and uncouth Behmenese.  Like John Bunyan, but never with John Bunyan's literary grace, Behmen will borrow, now a Latin word or phrase from his reading of learned authors, or, more often, from the conversations of his learned friends; and then he will take some astrological or alchemical expression of AGRIPPA, or PARACELSUS, or some such outlaw, and will, as with his awl and rosin-end, sew together a sentence, and hammer together a page of the most incongruous and unheard- of phraseology, till, as we read Behmen's earlier work especially, we continually exclaim, O for a chapter of John Bunyan's clear, and sweet, and classical English!  The |*Aurora*| was written in a language, if writing and a language it can be called, that had never been seen written or heard spoken before, or has since, on the face of the earth.  And as our students learn Greek in order to read Homer and Plato and Paul and John, and Latin in order to read Virgil and Tacitus, and Italian to read Dante, and German to read Goethe, so William Law tells us that he learned Behmen's Behmenite High Dutch, and that too after he was an old man, in order that he might completely master the |*Aurora*| and its kindred books. And as our schoolboys laugh and jeer at the outlandish sounds of Greek and Latin and German, till they have learned to read and love the great authors who have written in those languages, so WESLEY, and

SOUTHEY, and even HALLAM himself, jest and flout and call names at Jacob Behmen, because they have not taken the trouble to learn his language, to master his mind, and to drink in his spirit. At the same time, and after all that has been said about Behmen's barbarous style, Bishop Martensen tells us how the readers of SCHELLING were surprised and enraptured by a wealth of new expressions and new turns of speech in their mother tongue. But all these belonged to Behmen, or were fashioned on the model of his symbolical language. As it is, with all his astrology, and all his alchemy, and all his barbarities of form and expression, I for one will always take sides with the author of |*The Serious Call*|, and |*The Spirit of Prayer*|, and |*The Spirit of Love*|, and |*The Way to Divine Knowledge*|, in the disputed matter of Jacob Behmen's sanity and sanctity; and I will continue to believe that if I had only had the scholarship, and the intellect, and the patience, and the enterprise, to have mastered, through all their intricacies, the Behmenite grammar and the Behmenite vocabulary, I also would have found in Behmen all that Freher and Pordage and Law and Walton found. Even in the short way into this great man that I have gone, I have come upon such rare and rich mines of divine and eternal truth that I can easily believe that they who have dug deeper have come upon uncounted riches. 'Next to the Scriptures,' writes William Law, 'my only book is the illuminated Behmen. For the whole kingdom of grace and nature was opened in him. In reading Behmen I am always at home, and kept close to the kingdom of GOD that is within me.' 'I am not young,' said CLAUDE DE ST. MARTIN, 'being now near my fiftieth year, nevertheless I have begun to learn German, in order that I may read this incomparable author in his own tongue. I have written some not unacceptable books myself, but I am not worthy to unloose the shoestrings of this wonderful man. I advise you to throw yourself into the depths of Jacob Behmen. There is such a profundity and exaltation of truth in them, and such a simple and delicious nutriment.'

The Town Council of Goerlitz, hounded on by their Minister, sentenced Behmen to be banished, and interdicted him from ever writing any more. But in sheer shame at what they had done they immediately recalled Behmen from banishment; only, they insisted that he should confine himself to his shop, and leave all writing of books alone. Behmen had no ambition to write any more, and, as a matter of fact, he kept silence even to himself for seven whole years. But as those years went on it came to be with him, to use his own words, as with so much grain that has been buried in the earth, and which, in spite of storms and tempests, will, out of its own life, spring up, and that even when reason says it is now winter, and that all hope and all power is gone. And thus it was that, under the same instigation which had produced the *Aurora*, Behmen at a rush wrote his very fine if very difficult book, *The Three Principles of the Divine Essence*. He calls *The Three Principles* his A B C, and the easiest of all his books. And William Law recommends all beginners in Behmen to read alone for some sufficient time the tenth and twelfth chapters of *The Three Principles*. I shall let Behmen describe the contents of his easiest book in his own words. 'In this second book,' he says, 'there is declared what GOD is, what Nature is, what the creatures are, what the love and meekness of GOD are, what GOD'S will is, what the wrath of GOD is, and what joy and sorrow are. As also, how all things took their beginning: with the true difference between eternal and transitory creatures. Specially of man and his soul, what the soul is, and how it is an eternal creature. Also what heaven is, wherein GOD and the holy angels and holy men dwell, and hell wherein the devils dwell: and how all things were originally created and had their being. In sum, what the Essence of all Essences is. And thus I commit my reader to the sweet love of GOD.' |*The Three Principles*|, according to CHRISTOPHER WALTON, was the first book of Behmen's that William Law ever held in his hand. That, then, was the title-page, and those were the contents, that threw that princely and saintly mind into such a sweat. It was a great day for William Law, and through him it was, and will yet be acknowledged to have been, a great day for English theology when he chanced, at an old bookstall, upon |*The Three Principles*|, Englished by a Barrister of the Inner Temple. The picture of that bookstall that day is engraven in lines of light and love on the heart of every grateful reader of Jacob Behmen and of William Law's later and richer and riper writings.

In three months after he had finished |*The Three Principles*|, Behmen had composed a companion treatise, entitled |*The Threefold Life of Man*|. Modest about himself as Behmen always was, he could not be wholly blind about his own incomparable books. And he but spoke the simple truth about his third book when he said of it--as, indeed, he was constantly saying about all his books--that it will serve every reader just according to his constellation, his inclination, his disposition, his complexion, his profession, and his whole condition. 'You will be soon weary of all contentious books,' he wrote to CASPER LINDERN, 'if you entertain and get |*The Threefold Life of Man*| into your mind and heart.' 'The subject of regeneration,' says Christopher Walton, 'is the pith and drift of all Behmen's writings, and the student may here be directed to begin his course of study by mastering the first eight chapters of |*The Threefold Life*|, which appear to have been in great favour with Mr. Law.'

Behmen's next book was a very extraordinary piece of work, and it had a very extraordinary origin. A certain BALTHAZAR WALTER, who seems to have been a second Paracelsus in his love of knowledge and in his lifelong pursuit of knowledge, had, like Paracelsus, travelled east, and west, and north, and south in search of that ancient and occult wisdom of which so many men in that day dreamed. But Walter, like his predecessor Paracelsus, had come home from his travels a humbler man, a wiser man, and a man more ready to learn and lay to heart the truth that some of his own countrymen could all the time have taught him. On his return from the east, Walter found the name of Jacob Behmen in everybody's mouth; and, on introducing himself to that little shop in Goerlitz out of which the |*Aurora*| and |*The Threefold Life*| had come, Walter was wise enough to see and bold enough to confess that he had found a teacher and a friend there such as neither Egypt nor India had provided him with. After many immensely interested visits to Jacob Behmen's workshop, Walter was more than satisfied that Behmen was all, and more than all, that his most devoted admirers had said he was. And, accordingly, Walter laid a plan so as to draw upon Behmen's profound and original mind for a solution of some of the philosophical and theological problems that were agitating and dividing the learned men of that day. With that view Walter made a round of the leading universities of Germany, conversed with the professors and students, collected a long list of the questions that were being debated in that day in those seats of learning, and sent the list to Behmen, asking him to give his mind to them and try to answer them. 'Beloved sir,' wrote Behmen, after three months' meditation and prayer, 'and my good friend: it is impossible for the mind and reason of man to answer all the questions you have put to me. All those things are known to GOD alone. But, that no man may boast, He sometimes makes use of very mean men to make known His truth, that it may be seen and acknowledged to come from His own hand alone.' It is told that when Charles the First read the English translation of Behmen's answers to the |*Forty Questions*|, he wrote to the publisher that if Jacob Behmen was no scholar, then the Holy Ghost was still with men; and, if he was a learned man, then his book was one of the best inventions that had ever been written. The |*Forty Questions*| ran through many editions both on the Continent and in England, and it was this book that gained for Jacob Behmen the denomination of the Teutonic Philosopher, a name by which he is distinguished among authors to this day. The following are some of the university questions that Balthazar Walter took down and sent to Jacob Behmen for his answer: 'What is the soul of man in its innermost essence, and how is it created, soul by soul, in the image of GOD? Is the soul propagated from father to son like the body? or is it every time new created and breathed in from GOD? How comes original sin into each several soul? How does the soul of the saint feed and grow upon the word of GOD? Whence comes the deadly contrariety between the flesh and the spirit? Whither goes the soul when it at death departs from the body? In what does its rest, its awakening, and its glorification consist? What kind of body shall the glorified body be? The soul and spirit of CHRIST, what are they? and are they the same as ours? What and where is Paradise?' Through a hundred and fourteen large quarto pages Behmen's astonishing answers to the forty questions run; after which he adds this: 'Thus, my beloved friend, we have set down, according to our gifts, a round answer to your questions, and we exhort you as a brother not to despise us. For we are not born of art, but of simplicity. We acknowledge all who love such knowledge as our brethren in CHRIST, with whom we hope to rejoice eternally in the heavenly school. For our best knowledge here is but in part, but when we shall attain to perfection, then we shall see what GOD is, and what He can do. Amen.'

|A Treatise of the Incarnation of the Son of God| comes next, and

then we have three smaller works written to clear up and to establish several difficult and disputed matters in it and in some of his former works. To write on the Incarnation of the Son of GOD would need, says Behmen, an angel's pen; but his defence is that his is better than any angel's pen, because it is the pen of a sinner's love. The year 1621 saw one of Behmen's most original and most powerful books finished,-- the |*Signatura Rerum*|. In this remarkable book Behmen teaches us that all things have two worlds in which they live,--an inward world and an outward. All created things have an inner and an invisible essence, and an outer and a visible form. And the outward form is always more or less the key to the inward character. This whole world that we see around us, and of which we ourselves are the soul,--it is all a symbol, a 'signature,' of an invisible world.

This deep principle runs through the whole of creation. The Creator went upon this principle in all His work; and the thoughtful mind can see that principle coming out in all His work,--in plants, and trees, and beasts.

As German Boehme never cared for plants
Until it happed, a-walking in the fields,
He noticed all at once that plants could speak,
Nay, turned with loosened tongue to talk with him.
That day the daisy had an eye indeed--
Colloquized with the cowslips on such themes!
We find them extant yet in Jacob's prose.

But, best of all, this principle comes out clearest in the speech, behaviour, features, and face of a man. Every day men are signing themselves from within. Every act they perform, every word they speak, every wish they entertain,--it all comes out and is fixed for ever in their character, and even in their appearance. 'Therefore,' says Behmen in the beginning of his book, 'the greatest understanding lies in the signature. For by the external form of all creatures; by their voice and action, as well as by their instigation, inclination, and desire, their hidden spirit is made known. For Nature has given to everything its own language according to its innermost essence. And this is the language of Nature, in which everything continually speaks, manifests, and declares itself for what it is,--so much so, that all that is spoken or written even about GOD, however true, if the writer or speaker has not the Divine Nature within himself, then all he says is dumb to me; he has not got the hammer in his hand that can strike my bell.'

|The Way to Christ| was Behmen's next book, and in the four precious treatises that compose that book our author takes an altogether new departure. In his |*Aurora*|, in |*The Three Principles*|, in the |*Forty Questions*|, and in the |*Signatura Rerum*|, Jacob Behmen has been writing for philosophers and theologians. Or, if in all these works he has been writing for a memorial to himself in the first place,--even then, it has been for himself on the philosophical and theological side of his own mind. But in |*The Way to Christ*| he writes for himself under that character which, once taken up by Jacob Behmen, is never for one day laid down. Behmen's favourite Scripture, after our Lord's promise of the Holy Spirit to them that ask for Him, was the parable of the Prodigal Son. In all his books Behmen is that son, covered with wounds and bruises and putrefying sores, but at last beginning to come to himself and to return to his Father. |*The Way to Christ*| is a production of the very greatest depth and strength, but it is the depth and the strength of the heart and the conscience rather than the depth and the strength of the understanding and the imagination. This nobly evangelical book is made up of four tracts, entitled respectively, |*Of True Repentance*|,

*Of True Resignation*, *Of Regeneration*, and *Of the Supersensual Life*. And a deep vein of autobiographic life and interest runs through the four tracts and binds them into a quick unity. 'A soldier,' says Behmen, 'who has been in the wars can best tell another soldier how to fight.' And neither Augustine nor Luther nor Bunyan carries deeper wounds, or broader scars, nor tells a nobler story in any of their autobiographic and soldierly books than Behmen does in his *Way to Christ*. At the commencement of *The True Repentance* he promises us that he will write of a process or way on which he himself has gone. 'The author herewith giveth thee the best jewel that he hath.' And a true jewel it is, as the present speaker will testify. If *The True Repentance* has a fault at all it is the fault of Rutherford's *Letters*. For the taste of some of his readers Behmen, like Rutherford, draws rather too much on the language and the figures of the married life in setting forth the love of CHRIST to the espoused soul, and the love of the espoused soul to CHRIST. But with that, and all its other drawbacks, *The True Repentance* is such a treatise that, once discovered by the proper reader, it will be the happy discoverer's constant companion all his earthly and penitential days. As the English reader is carried on through the fourth tract, *The Supersensual Life*, he experiences a new and an increasing sense of ease and pleasure, combined with a mystic height and depth and inwardness all but new to him even in Behmen's books. The new height and depth and inwardness are all Jacob Behmen's own; but the freedom and the ease and the movement and the melody are all William Law's. In his preparations for a new edition of Behmen in English, William Law had re-translated and paraphrased *The Supersensual Life*, and the editor of the 1781 edition of Behmen's works has incorporated Law's beautiful rendering of that tract in room of JOHN SPARROW'S excellent but rather too antique rendering. We are in John Sparrow's everlasting debt for the immense labour he laid out on Behmen, as well as for his own deep piety and personal worth. But it was service enough and honour enough for Sparrow to have Englished Jacob Behmen at all for his fellow-countrymen, even if he was not able to English him as William Law would have done. But take Behmen and Law together, as they meet together in |*The Supersensual Life*|, and not A Kempis himself comes near them even in his own proper field, or in his immense service in that field. There is all the reality, inwardness, and spirituality of |*The Imitation*| in |*The Supersensual Life*|, together with a sweep of imagination, and a grasp of understanding, as well as with both a sweetness and a bitterness of heart that even A Kempis never comes near. |*The Supersensual Life*| of Jacob Behmen, in the English of William Law, is a superb piece of spiritual work, and a treasure-house of masculine English. (If Christopher Walton is right, we must read 'Lee' for 'Law' in this passage. If Walton is right, then there was a master of English in those days we had not before been told of.)

|A Treatise of the Four Complexions|, or |*A Consolatory Instruction for a Sad and Assaulted Heart*|, was Behmen's next book. The four complexions are the four temperaments--the choleric, the sanguine, the phlegmatic, and the melancholy. Behmen's treatise has been well described by Walton as containing the philosophy of temptation; and by Martensen as displaying a most profound knowledge of the human heart. Behmen sets about his task as a |*ductor dubitantium*| in a masterly manner. He takes in hand the comfort and direction of sin-distressed souls in a characteristically deep, inward, and thorough-going way. The book is full of Behmen's observation of men. It is the outcome of a close and long-continued study of character and conduct. Every page of |*The Four Complexions*| gleams with a keen but tender and wistful insight into our poor human nature. As his customers came and gave

their orders in his shop; as his neighbours collected, and gossiped, and debated, and quarrelled around his shop window; as his minister fumed and raged against him in the pulpit; as the Council of Goerlitz sat and swayed, passed sentence upon him, retracted their sentence, and again gave way under the pressure of their minister, and pronounced another sentence,--all this time Behmen was having poor human nature, to all its joints and marrow, and to all the thoughts and instincts of its heart, laid naked and open before him, both in other men and in himself. And then, as always with Behmen, all this observation of men, all this discovery and self-discovery, ran up into philosophy, into theology, into personal and evangelical religion. In all that Behmen better and better saw the original plan, constitution, and operation of human nature; its aboriginal catastrophe; its weakness and openness to all evil; and its need of constant care, protection, instruction, watchfulness, and Divine help. Behmen writes on all the four temperaments with the profoundest insight, and with the fullest sympathy; but over the last of the four he exclaims: 'O hear me! for I know well myself what melancholy is! I also have lodged all my days in the melancholy inn!' As I read that light and elastic book published the other day, |*The Life and Letters of Erasmus*|, I came on this sentence, 'Erasmus, like all men of real genius, had a light and elastic nature.' When I read that, I could not believe my eyes. I had been used to think of light and elastic natures as being the antipodes of natures of real genius. And as I stopped my reading for a little, a procession of men of real and indisputable genius passed before me, who had all lodged with Behmen in the melancholy inn. Till I remembered that far deeper and far truer saying, that 'simply to say man at all is to say melancholy.' No: with all respect, the real fact is surely as near as possible the exact opposite. A light, elastic, Erasmus- like nature, is the exception among men of real genius. At any rate, Jacob Behmen was the exact opposite of Erasmus, and of all such light and elastic men. Melancholy was Jacob Behmen's special temperament and peculiar complexion. He had long studied, and watched, and wrestled with, and prayed over that complexion at home. And thus it is, no doubt, that he is so full, and so clear, and so sure-footed, and so impressive, and so full of fellow-feeling in his treatment of this special complexion. Behmen's greatest disciple has assimilated his master's teaching in this matter of complexion also, and has given it out again in his own clear, plain, powerful, classical manner, especially in his treatise on |*Christian Regeneration*|. Let all preachers and pastors who would master the |*rationale*| of temptation, and who would ground their directions and their comforts to their people in the nature of things, as well as in the word of GOD, make Jacob Behmen and William Law and Prebendary Clark their constant study. 'I write for no other purpose,' says Behmen, 'than that men may learn how to know themselves. Seek the noble knowledge of thyself. Seek it and you will find a heavenly treasure which will not be eaten by moths, and which no thief shall ever take away.'

I shall not attempt to enter on the thorny thicket of Jacob Behmen's polemical and apologetical works. I shall not even load your mind with their unhappy titles. His five apologies occupy in bulk somewhere about a tenth part of his five quarto volumes. And full as his apologies and defences are of autobiographic material, as well as of valuable expansions and explanations of his other books, yet at their best they are all controversial and combative in their cast and complexion; and, nobly as Behmen has written on the subject of controversy, it was not given even to him, amid all the misunderstandings, misrepresentations, injuries, and insults he suffered from, always to write what we are glad and proud and the better to read.

About his next book Behmen thus writes: 'Upon the desire of some high persons with whom I did converse in the Christmas holidays, I have written a pretty large treatise upon Election, in which I have done my best to determine that subject upon the deepest grounds. And I hope that the same may put an end to many contentions and controversies, especially of some points betwixt the Lutherans and Calvinists, for I have taken the texts of Holy Scripture which speak of GOD'S will to harden sinners, and then, again, of His unwillingness to harden, and have so tuned and harmonised them that the right understanding and meaning of the same may be seen.' 'This author,' says John Sparrow, 'disputes not at all. He desires only to confer and offer his understanding of the Scriptures on both sides, answering reason's objections, and manifesting the truth for the conjoining, uniting, and reconciling of all parties in love.' And that he has not been wholly unsuccessful we may believe when we hear one of Behmen's ablest commentators writing of his |*Election*| as 'a superlatively helpful book,' and again, as a 'profoundly instructive treatise.' The workman-like way in which Behmen sets about his treatment of the |*Election of Grace, commonly called Predestination*|, will be seen from the titles of some of his chapters. Chap. i. What the One Only GOD is. Chap. ii. Concerning GOD'S Eternal Speaking Word. Chap. v. Of the Origin of Man; Chap. vi. Of the Fall of Man. Chap. viii. Of the sayings of Scripture, and how they oppose one another. Chap. ix. Clearing the Right Understanding of such Scriptures. Chap. xiii. A Conclusion upon all those Questions. And then, true to his constant manner, as if wholly dissatisfied with the result of all his labour in things and in places too deep both for writer and reader, he gave all the next day after he had finished his |*Election*| to an |*Appendix on Repentance*|, in order to making his own and his reader's calling and election sure. And it may safely be said that, than that day's work, than those four quarto pages, not Augustine, not Luther, not Bunyan, not Baxter, not Shepard has ever written anything of more evangelical depth, and strength, and passion, and pathos. It is truly a splendid day's work! But it might not have been possible even for Behmen to perform that day's work had he not for months beforehand been dealing day and night with the deepest and the most heart-searching things both of GOD and man. What a man was Jacob Behmen, and chosen to what a service! At work all that day in his solitary stall, and then all the night after over his rush-light writing for a memorial to himself and to us his incomparable |*Compendium of Repentance*|.

In a letter addressed to one of the nobility in Silesia, and dated February 19, 1623, Behmen says: 'When you have leisure to study I shall send you something still more deep, for I have written this whole autumn and winter without ceasing.' And if he had written nothing else but his great book entitled |*Mysterium Magnum*| that autumn and winter, he must have written night and day and done nothing else. Even in size the |*Mysterium*| is an immense piece of work. In the English edition it occupies the whole of the third quarto volume of 507 pages; and then for its matter it is a still more amazing production. To say that the |*Mysterium Magnum*| is a mystical and allegorical commentary upon the Book of Genesis is to say nothing. Philo himself is a tyro and a timid interpreter beside Jacob Behmen. 'Which things are an allegory,' says the Apostle, after a passing reference to Sarah and Hagar and Isaac and Ishmael; but if you would see actually every syllable of Genesis allegorised, spiritualised, interpreted of CHRIST, and of the New Testament, from the first verse of its first chapter to the last verse of its last chapter, like the nobleman of Silesia, when you have leisure, read Behmen's deep |*Mysterium Magnum*|. I would recommend the enterprising and unconquerable student to make leisure so as to master Behmen's Preface to the |*Mysterium Magnum*| at the very least. And if he does that, and is not drawn on from that to be a student of Behmen for the rest of his days, then, whatever else his proper field in life may be, it is not mystical or philosophical theology. It is a long step both in time and in thought from Behmen to SCHOPENHAUER; but, speaking of one of Schelling's books, Schopenhauer says that it is all taken from Jacob Behmen's |*Mysterium Magnum*|; every thought and almost every word of Schelling's work leads Schopenhauer to think of Behmen. 'When I read Behmen's book,' says Schopenhauer, 'I cannot withhold either admiration or emotion.' At his far too early death Behmen left four treatises behind him in an unfinished condition. The |*Theoscopia*|, or |*Divine Vision*|, is but a fragment; but, even so, the study of that fragment leads us to believe that, had Behmen lived to the ordinary limit of human life, and had his mind continued to grow as it was now fast growing in clearness, in concentration, and in simplicity, Behmen would have left to us not a few books as classical in their form as all his books are classical in their substance; in their originality, in their truth, in their depth, and in their strength. As it is, the unfinished, the scarcely-begun, |*Theoscopia*| only serves to show the student of what a treasure he has been bereft by Behmen's too early death. As I read and re-read the |*Theoscopia*| I felt the full truth and force of Hegel's generous words, that German philosophy began with Behmen. This is both German and Christian philosophy, I said to myself as I revelled in the |*Theoscopia*|. Let the serious student listen to the titles of some of the chapters of the |*Theoscopia*|, and then let him say what he would not have given to have got such a book from such a pen in its completed shape: 'What GOD is, and how we men shall know the Divine Substance by the Divine Revelation. Why it sometimes seems as if there were no GOD, and as if all things went in the world by chance. Why GOD, who is Love itself, permits an evil will contrary to His own. The reason and the profit, why evil should be found along with good. Of the mind of man, and how it is the image of GOD, and how it can still be filled with God. Why this Temporal Universe is created; to what it is profitable; and how God is so near unto all things': and so on. 'But no amount of quotation,' says Mrs. Penney, that very able student of Behmen, lately deceased, 'can give an adequate glimpse of the light which streams from the |*Theoscopia*| when long and patiently studied.'

Another unfinished fragment that Behmen's readers seek for and treasure up like very sand of gold is his |*Holy Week*|. This little work, its author tells us, was undertaken upon the entreaty and desire of some loving and good friends of his for the daily exercise of true religion in their hearts and in the little church of their families. The following is Behmen's method of prayer for Monday, which is the only day's prayer he got finished before his death: 'A short prayer when we awake early and before we rise. A prayer and thanksgiving after we are risen. A prayer while we wash and dress. A prayer when we begin to work at our calling. A prayer at noon. A prayer toward evening. A prayer when we undress. A prayer of thanks for the bitter passion and dying of JESUS CHRIST.' What does the man mean? many of his contemporaries who came upon his |*Holy Week*| would say, What does the madman mean? Would he have us pray all day? Would he have us pray and do nothing else? Yes; it would almost seem so. For in his |*Supersensual Life*| the Master says to the disciple who has asked, 'How shall I be able to live aright amid all the anxiety and tribulation of this world?': 'If thou dost once every hour throw thyself by faith beyond all creatures into the abysmal mercy of GOD, into the sufferings of CHRIST, and into the fellowship of His intercession, then thou shalt receive power from above to rule over the world, and death, and the devil, and hell itself.' And again, 'O thou of little courage, if thy will could but break itself off every half-hour from all creatures, and plunge itself into that where no creature is or can be, presently it would be penetrated with the splendour of the Divine glory, and would taste a sweetness no tongue can express. Then thou wouldst love thy cross more than all the glory and all the goods of this world.' The author had begun a series of reflections and meditations on the Ten Commandments for devotional use on Tuesday, but got no further than the Fifth. Behmen is so deep and so original in his purely philosophical, theological, and speculative books, that in many places we can only stand back and wonder at the man. But in his |*Holy Week*| Behmen kneels down beside us. Not but that his characteristic depth is present in his prayers also; but we all know something of the nature, the manner, and the blessedness of prayer, and thus it is that we are so much more at home with Behmen, the prodigal son, than we are with Behmen, the theosophical theologian. When Behmen begins to teach us to pray, and when the lesson comes to us out of his own closet, then we are able to see in a nearer light something of the originality, the greatness, the strength, and the true and genuine piety of the philosopher and the theologian. When Behmen's philosophy and theology become penitence, prayer, and praise, then by their fruits we know how good his philosophy and his theology must be, away down in their deepest and most hidden nature. I agree with Walton that those prayers are full of unction and instruction, and that some of them are of the 'highest magnetical power'; and that, as rendered into modern phraseology, they are most beautiful devotional compositions, and very models of all that a divinely illuminated mind would address to GOD and CHRIST. For myself, immediately after the Psalms of David I put Jacob Behmen's |*Holy Week*| and the prayers scattered up and down through his |*True Repentance*|, and beside Behmen I put Bishop Andrewes' |*Private Devotions*|. I have discovered no helps to my own devotional life for a moment to set beside Behmen and Andrewes.

|A Treatise on Baptism and the Lord's Supper|; |*A Key to the Principal Points and Expressions in the Author's Writings*|; and then a most valuable volume of letters--|Epistolae Theosophicae|--complete the extraordinarily rich bibliography of the illuminated and blessed Jacob Behmen.

Though there is a great deal of needless and wearisome repetition in Jacob Behmen's writings, at the same time there is scarcely a single subject in the whole range of theology on which he does not throw a new, an intense, and a brilliant light. In his absolutely original and magnificent doctrine of GOD, while all the time loyally true to it, Behmen has confessedly transcended the theology of both the Latin and the Reformed Churches; and, absolutely unlettered man though he is, has taken his stand at the very head of the great Greek theologians. The Reformers concentrated their criticism upon the anthropology and soteriology of the Church of Rome, and especially upon the discipline and worship connected therewith. They saw no need for recasting any of the more fundamental positions of pure theology. And while Jacob Behmen, broadly speaking, accepts as his own confession of faith all that Luther and Calvin and their colleagues taught on sin and salvation, on the corruption and guilt of sinners, and on the redeeming work of our LORD, he rises far above the greatest and best of his teachers in his doctrine of the GODHEAD. Not only does he rise far higher in that doctrine than either Rome or Geneva, he rises far higher and sounds far deeper than either Antioch, or Alexandria, or Nicomedia, or Nice. On this profound point Bishop Martensen has an excellent appreciation of Behmen. After what I have taken upon me to say about Behmen, the learned Bishop's authoritative passage must be quoted:--'If we compare Behmen's doctrine of the Trinity,' says the learned and evangelical

Bishop, 'with that which is contained in the otherwise so admirable Athanasian Creed, the latter but displays to us a most abstruse metaphysic; a GOD for mere thought, and in whom there is nothing sympathetic for the heart of man. Behmen, on the contrary, reveals to us the LIVING GOD, the GOD of Goodness, the Eternal Love, of which there is absolutely no hint whatever in the hard Athanasian symbol. By this attitude of his to the affections of the human heart, Behmen's doctrine of the Trinity is in close coherence with the Reformation, and with its evangelical churches. . . . Behmen is anxious to state a conception of GOD that will fill the hiatus between the theological and anthropological sides of the dogmatical development which was bequeathed by the Reformation; he seeks to unite the theological and the anthropological. . . . From careful study of Behmen's theology,' continues Bishop Martensen, 'one gains a prevailing impression that Behmen's GOD is, in His inmost Being, most kindred to man, even as man in his inmost being is still kindred to GOD. And, besides, we recognise in Behmen throughout the pulse-beat of a believing man, who is in all his books supremely anxious about his own salvation and that of his fellow-men.' Now, it is just this super-confessional element in Behmen, both on his speculative and on his practical side, taken along with the immediate and intensely practical bearing of all his speculations, it is just this that is Behmen's true and genuine distinction, his shining and unshared glory. And it is out of that supreme, solitary, and wholly untrodden field of Behmen's super-confessional theology that all that is essential, characteristic, distinctive, and fruitful in Behmen really and originally springs. The distinctions he takes within, and around, and immediately beneath the Godhead, are of themselves full of the noblest light. The Divine Nature, Eternal Nature, Temporal Nature, Human Nature, when evolved out of one another, and when related to one another, as Behmen sees them evolved and related, are categories of the clearest, surest, most necessary, and most intensely instructive kind. And if the height and the depth, the massiveness, the stupendousness, and the grandeur, as well as the sweetness, and the beauty, and the warmth, and the fruitfulness of a doctrine of GOD is any argument or evidence of its truth, then Behmen's magnificent doctrine of the GODHEAD is surely proved to demonstration and delight. GOD is the Essence of all Essences to Behmen. GOD is the deepest Ground, the living and the life-giving Root of all existence. At the same time, the Divine Nature is so Divine; It is so high and so deep; It is so unlike all that is not Itself; It is so beyond and above all language, and all thought, and all imagination of man or angel, that universe after universe have had to come into existence, and have had to be filled, each successive universe after its own kind, with all the fulness of GOD, before that universe of which we form a part, and to which our utmost imagination is confined, could have come into existence, and into recognition of itself. Behmen's Eternal Nature must never be taken for the Eternal GOD. The Divine Nature, the Eternal Godhead, exists in the Father, in the Son, and in the Holy Ghost; and then, after the Eternal Generation of the Son, and the Eternal Procession of the Holy Ghost, there comes up in order of existence Eternal Nature. Eternal Nature is not the Divine Nature, but it is as near to the Divine Nature in its qualities and in its powers as any created thing can ever by any possibility be. Now, if we are still to follow Behmen, we must not let ourselves indolently think of the production of Eternal Nature as a divine act done and completed in any past either of time or of eternity. There is neither past nor future where we are now walking with Behmen. There is only an everlasting present where he is now leading us. For, as GOD the Father generates the Son eternally and continually; and as the Holy Ghost proceeds from the Father and the

Son eternally and continually, so GOD the Word eternally and continually says, 'Let this Beginning of all things be, and let it continue to be.' And, as He speaks, His Word awakens the ever-dawning morning of the ever new-created day. And He beholds Eternal Nature continually rising up before Him, and He pronounces it very good. The Creator so transcends the creation, and, especially, that late and remote creation of which we are a part, that, as the Creator's first step out of Himself, and as a step towards our creation, is His creation, generation, or other production of a nature or universe that shall be capable of receiving immediately into itself all that of the Creator that He has purposed to reveal and to communicate to creatures,--a nature or universe which shall at the same time be itself the beginning of creation, and the source, spring, and quarry out of which all that shall afterwards come can be constructed. Eternal Nature is thus the great storehouse and workshop in which all the created essences, elements, principles, and potentialities of all possible worlds are laid up. Here is the great treasury and laboratory into which the Filial Word enters, when by Him GOD creates, sustains, and perfects the worlds, universe after universe. Here, says Behmen, is the great and universal treasury of that heavenly clay of which all things, even to angels and men, are made; and here is the eternal turning-wheel with which they are all framed and fashioned. Eternal Nature is an invisible essence, and it is the essential ground out of which all the visible and invisible worlds are made. For the things which are seen were not made of things which do appear. In that radiant original universe also all the thoughts of GOD which were to us-ward from everlasting, all the Divine ideas, patterns, and plans of things, are laid open, displayed, copied out and sealed up for future worlds to see carried out. 'Through this Kingdom of Heaven, or Eternal Nature,' says William Law, in his |*Appeal to all that Doubt*|, 'is the invisible GOD eternally breaking forth and manifesting Himself in a boundless height and depth of blissful wonders, opening and displaying Himself to all His heavenly creatures in an infinite variety and an endless multiplicity of His powers, beauties, joys, and glories. So that all the inhabitants of heaven are for ever knowing, seeing, hearing, feeling, and variously enjoying all that is great, amiable, infinite, and gracious in the Divine Nature.' And again, in his |*Way to Divine Knowledge*|: 'Out of this transcendent Eternal Nature, which is as universal and immense as the Godhead itself, do all the highest beings, cherubims and seraphims, all the hosts of angels, and all intelligent spirits, receive their birth, existence, substance, and form. And they are one and united in one, GOD in them, and they in GOD, according to the prayer of CHRIST for His disciples, that they, and He, and His Holy Father might be united in one.' A little philosophy, especially when the philosopher does not yet know the plague of his own heart, tends, indeed, to doubt and unbelief in the word of GOD and in the work of CHRIST. But the philosophy of Behmen and Law will deepen the mind and subdue the heart of the student till he is made a prodigal son, a humble believer, and a profound philosopher, both in nature and in grace, like his profound masters.

Behmen's teaching on human nature, his doctrine of the heart of man, and of the image of GOD in the heart of man, has a greatness about it that marks it off as being peculiarly Behmen's own doctrine. He agrees with the catechisms and the creeds in their teaching that the heart of man was at first like the heart of GOD in knowledge, righteousness, and true holiness. But Behmen is above and beyond the catechisms in this also, in the way that he sees the heart of man still opening in upon the Divine Nature, as also upon Eternal and Temporal Nature, somewhat as the heart of GOD opens on all that He has made. On every page of his, wherever you happen to open him, Behmen is found teaching that GOD and CHRIST, heaven and hell, life and death, are in every several human heart. Heaven and all that it contains is every day either being quenched and killed in every human heart, or it is being anew generated, rekindled, and accepted there; and in like manner hell. 'Yea,' he is bold to exclaim, 'GOD Himself is so near thee that the geniture of the Holy Trinity is continually being wrought in thy heart. Yea, all the Three Persons are generated for thee in thy heart.' And, again: 'GOD is in thy dark heart. Knock, and He shall come out within thee into the light. The Holy Ghost holds the key of thy dark heart. Ask, and He shall be given to thee within thee. Do not let any sophister teach thee that thy GOD is far aloft from thee as the stars are. Only offer at this moment to GOD thine heart, and CHRIST, the Son of GOD, will be born and formed within thee. And then thou art His brother, His flesh, and His spirit. Thou also art a child of His Father. GOD is in thee. Power, might, majesty, heaven, paradise, elements, stars, the whole earth--all is thine. Thou art in CHRIST over hell, and all that it contains.' 'Behmen's speculation,' Martensen is always reminding us, 'streams forth from the deepest practical inspiration. His speculations are all saturated with a constant reference to salvation. His whole metaphysic is pervaded by practical applications.' And conspicuously so, we may here point out, is his metaphysic of GOD and of the heart of man. The immanence of GOD, as theologians and philosophers call it; the indwelling of GOD, as the psalmists and the apostles and the saints call it; the Divine Word lightening every man that comes into the world, as John has it,--of the practical and personal bearings of all that Behmen's every book is full. Dost thou not see it and feel it? he continually calls to his readers. Heaven, be sure, is in every holy man, and hell in every bad man. When thou dost work together with GOD then thou art in heaven, and thy soul dwells in GOD. In like manner, also, thou art in hell and among the devils when thou art in any envy, malice, anger, or ill-will. Thou needest not to ask where is heaven or where is hell. Both are within thee, even in thy heart. Now, then, when thou prayest, pray in that heaven that is within thee, and there the Holy Ghost shall meet with thee and will help thee, and thy soul shall be the whole of heaven within thee. It is a fundamental doctrine of Behmen's that the fall would have been immediate and eternal death to Adam and Eve had not the Divine Word, the Seed of the woman, entered their hearts, and kept a footing in their hearts, and in the hearts of all their children, against the fulness of time when He would take our flesh and work out our redemption. And thus it is that Behmen appeals to all his readers, that if they will only go down deep enough into their own hearts--then, there, down there, deeper than indwelling sin, deeper than original sin, deep down and seated in the very substance and centre of their souls--they will come upon secret and unexpected seeds of the Divine Life. Seeds, blades, buddings, and new beginnings of the very life of GOD the Son, in their deepest souls. Secret and small, Behmen exclaims, as those seeds of Eden are, despise them not; destroy them not, for a blessing for thee is in them. Water those secret seeds, sun them, dig about them, and they will grow up in you also. The Divine Life is in you, quench it not, for it is of GOD. Nay, it is GOD Himself in you. It depends upon yourself whether or no that which is at this moment the smallest of all seeds is yet to become in you the greatest and the most fruitful of all trees.

'Man never knows how anthropomorphic he is,' is a characteristic saying of a fellow-countryman of Behmen's. And Behmen's super-confessional and almost super-scriptural treatment of that frequent scriptural anthropomorphism,--'unavoidable and yet intolerable,'--the wrath of GOD, must be left by me in Behmen's own bold pages. Strong meat belongeth to them that are of full age, even those who by reason of use have their senses exercised to discern both good and evil. Behmen's philosophical, theological, and experimental doctrine of sin also, with one example, must be wholly passed by. 'If all trees were clerks,' he exclaims in one place, 'and all their branches pens, and all the hills books, and all the water ink, yet all would not sufficiently declare the evil that sin hath done. For sin has made this house of heavenly light to be a den of darkness; this house of joy to be a house of mourning, lamentation, and woe; this house of all refreshment to be full of hunger and thirst; this abode of love to be a prison of enmity and ill-will; this seat of meekness to be the haunt of pride and rage and malice. For laughter sin has brought horror; for munificence, beggary; and for heaven, hell. Oh, thou miserable man, turn convert. For the Father stretches out both His hands to thee. Do but turn to Him and He will receive and embrace thee in His love.' It was the sin and misery of this world that first made Jacob Behmen a philosopher, and it was the sinfulness of his own heart that at last made him a saint. Behmen's full doctrine and practice of prayer also; his fine and fruitful treatment of what he always calls 'the process of CHRIST'; and, intimately connected with that, his still super-confessional treatment of imputation,--of all that, and much more like that, I cannot now attempt to speak. Nor yet of his superb teaching on love. 'Throw out thy heart upon all men,' he now commands and now beseeches us. 'Throw open and throw out thy heart. For unless thou dost exercise thy heart, and the love of thy heart, upon every man in the world, thy self-love, thy pride, thy contempt, thy envy, thy distaste, thy dislike will still have dominion over thee. The Divine Nature will be quenched and extinguished in thee, till nothing but self and hell is left to thee. In the name, and in the strength of GOD, love all men. Love thy neighbour as thyself, and do to thy neighbour as thou doest to thyself. And do it now. For now is the accepted time; and now is the day of salvation!'

Jacob Behmen died in his fiftieth year. He was libelled and maligned, harassed and hunted to death by a world that was not worthy of such a gift of GOD. A sudden and severe sickness came upon Behmen till he sank in death with his |*Aurora*| and his |*Holy Week*| and his |*Divine Vision*| all lying still unfinished at his bedside. 'Open the door and let in more of that music,' the dying man said to his weeping son. Behmen was already hearing the harpers harping with their harps. He was already taking his part in the song they sing in heaven to Him who loved them, and washed them from their sins in His own blood. 'And now,' said the prodigal son, the blessed Behmen, 'I go to-day to be with my Redeemer and my King in Paradise,' and so died.

www.bookjungle.com *email: sales@bookjungle.com fax: 630-214-0564 mail: Book Jungle PO Box 2226 Champaign, IL 61825*

### The Codes Of Hammurabi And Moses
### W. W. Davies

QTY

The discovery of the Hammurabi Code is one of the greatest achievements of archaeology, and is of paramount interest, not only to the student of the Bible, but also to all those interested in ancient history...

**Religion**   **ISBN:** *1-59462-338-4*   **Pages:132**
*MSRP $12.95*

### The Theory of Moral Sentiments
### Adam Smith

QTY

This work from 1749. contains original theories of conscience amd moral judgment and it is the foundation for systemof morals.

**Philosophy**   **ISBN:** *1-59462-777-0*   **Pages:536**
*MSRP $19.95*

### Jessica's First Prayer
### Hesba Stretton

QTY

In a screened and secluded corner of one of the many railway-bridges which span the streets of London there could be seen a few years ago, from five o'clock every morning until half past eight, a tidily set-out coffee-stall, consisting of a trestle and board, upon which stood two large tin cans, with a small fire of charcoal burning under each so as to keep the coffee boiling during the early hours of the morning when the work-people were thronging into the city on their way to their daily toil...

**Pages:84**

**Childrens**   **ISBN:** *1-59462-373-2*   *MSRP $9.95*

### My Life and Work
### Henry Ford

QTY

Henry Ford revolutionized the world with his implementation of mass production for the Model T automobile. Gain valuable business insight into his life and work with his own auto-biography... "We have only started on our development of our country we have not as yet, with all our talk of wonderful progress, done more than scratch the surface. The progress has been wonderful enough but..."

**Pages:300**

**Biographies/**   **ISBN:** *1-59462-198-5*   *MSRP $21.95*

www.bookjungle.com *email: sales@bookjungle.com fax: 630-214-0564 mail: Book Jungle PO Box 2226 Champaign, IL 61825*

### The Art of Cross-Examination
### Francis Wellman

QTY

I presume it is the experience of every author, after his first book is published upon an important subject, to be almost overwhelmed with a wealth of ideas and illustrations which could readily have been included in his book, and which to his own mind, at least, seem to make a second edition inevitable. Such certainly was the case with me; and when the first edition had reached its sixth impression in five months, I rejoiced to learn that it seemed to my publishers that the book had met with a sufficiently favorable reception to justify a second and considerably enlarged edition. ..

Reference    ISBN: *1-59462-647-2*    Pages:412   MSRP *$19.95*

### On the Duty of Civil Disobedience
### Henry David Thoreau

QTY

Thoreau wrote his famous essay, On the Duty of Civil Disobedience, as a protest against an unjust but popular war and the immoral but popular institution of slave-owning. He did more than write—he declined to pay his taxes, and was hauled off to gaol in consequence. Who can say how much this refusal of his hastened the end of the war and of slavery ?

Law    ISBN: *1-59462-747-9*    Pages:48    MSRP *$7.45*

### Dream Psychology Psychoanalysis for Beginners
### Sigmund Freud

QTY

Sigmund Freud, born Sigismund Schlomo Freud (May 6, 1856 - September 23, 1939), was a Jewish-Austrian neurologist and psychiatrist who co-founded the psychoanalytic school of psychology. Freud is best known for his theories of the unconscious mind, especially involving the mechanism of repression; his redefinition of sexual desire as mobile and directed towards a wide variety of objects; and his therapeutic techniques, especially his understanding of transference in the therapeutic relationship and the presumed value of dreams as sources of insight into unconscious desires.

Psychology    ISBN: *1-59462-905-6*    Pages:196    MSRP *$15.45*

### The Miracle of Right Thought
### Orison Swett Marden

QTY

Believe with all of your heart that you will do what you were made to do. When the mind has once formed the habit of holding cheerful, happy, prosperous pictures, it will not be easy to form the opposite habit. It does not matter how improbable or how far away this realization may see, or how dark the prospects may be, if we visualize them as best we can, as vividly as possible, hold tenaciously to them and vigorously struggle to attain them, they will gradually become actualized, realized in the life. But a desire, a longing without endeavor, a yearning abandoned or held indifferently will vanish without realization.

Self Help    ISBN: *1-59462-644-8*    Pages:360    MSRP *$25.45*

www.bookjungle.com  email: sales@bookjungle.com  fax: 630-214-0564  mail: Book Jungle  PO Box 2226  Champaign, IL 61825

QTY

| | Title | ISBN | Price |
|---|---|---|---|
| ☐ | **The Rosicrucian Cosmo-Conception Mystic Christianity** by *Max Heindel* | ISBN: 1-59462-188-8 | $38.95 |
| | *The Rosicrucian Cosmo-conception is not dogmatic, neither does it appeal to any other authority than the reason of the student. It is: not controversial, but is: sent forth in the, hope that it may help to clear...* | | New Age/Religion Pages 646 |
| ☐ | **Abandonment To Divine Providence** by *Jean-Pierre de Caussade* | ISBN: 1-59462-228-0 | $25.95 |
| | *"The Rev. Jean Pierre de Caussade was one of the most remarkable spiritual writers of the Society of Jesus in France in the 18th Century. His death took place at Toulouse in 1751. His works have gone through many editions and have been republished...* | | Inspirational/Religion Pages 400 |
| ☐ | **Mental Chemistry** by *Charles Haanel* | ISBN: 1-59462-192-6 | $23.95 |
| | *Mental Chemistry allows the change of material conditions by combining and appropriately utilizing the power of the mind. Much like applied chemistry creates something new and unique out of careful combinations of chemicals the mastery of mental chemistry...* | | New Age Pages 354 |
| ☐ | **The Letters of Robert Browning and Elizabeth Barret Barrett 1845-1846 vol II** by *Robert Browning* and *Elizabeth Barrett* | ISBN: 1-59462-193-4 | $35.95 |
| | | | Biographies Pages 596 |
| ☐ | **Gleanings In Genesis (volume I)** by *Arthur W. Pink* | ISBN: 1-59462-130-6 | $27.45 |
| | *Appropriately has Genesis been termed "the seed plot of the Bible" for in it we have, in germ form, almost all of the great doctrines which are afterwards fully developed in the books of Scripture which follow...* | | Religion/Inspirational Pages 420 |
| ☐ | **The Master Key** by *L. W. de Laurence* | ISBN: 1-59462-001-6 | $30.95 |
| | *In no branch of human knowledge has there been a more lively increase of the spirit of research during the past few years than in the study of Psychology, Concentration and Mental Discipline. The requests for authentic lessons in Thought Control, Mental Discipline and...* | | New Age/Business Pages 422 |
| ☐ | **The Lesser Key Of Solomon Goetia** by *L. W. de Laurence* | ISBN: 1-59462-092-X | $9.95 |
| | *This translation of the first book of the "Lernegton" which is now for the first time made accessible to students of Talismanic Magic was done, after careful collation and edition, from numerous Ancient Manuscripts in Hebrew, Latin, and French...* | | New Age/Occult Pages 92 |
| ☐ | **Rubaiyat Of Omar Khayyam** by *Edward Fitzgerald* | ISBN:1-59462-332-5 | $13.95 |
| | *Edward Fitzgerald, whom the world has already learned, in spite of his own efforts to remain within the shadow of anonymity, to look upon as one of the rarest poets of the century, was born at Bredfield, in Suffolk, on the 31st of March, 1809. He was the third son of John Purcell...* | | Music Pages 172 |
| ☐ | **Ancient Law** by *Henry Maine* | ISBN: 1-59462-128-4 | $29.95 |
| | *The chief object of the following pages is to indicate some of the earliest ideas of mankind, as they are reflected in Ancient Law, and to point out the relation of those ideas to modern thought.* | | Religion/History Pages 452 |
| ☐ | **Far-Away Stories** by *William J. Locke* | ISBN: 1-59462-129-2 | $19.45 |
| | *"Good wine needs no bush, but a collection of mixed vintages does. And this book is just such a collection. Some of the stories I do not want to remain buried for ever in the museum files of dead magazine-numbers an author's not unpardonable vanity..."* | | Fiction Pages 272 |
| ☐ | **Life of David Crockett** by *David Crockett* | ISBN: 1-59462-250-7 | $27.45 |
| | *"Colonel David Crockett was one of the most remarkable men of the times in which he lived. Born in humble life, but gifted with a strong will, an indomitable courage, and unremitting perseverance...* | | Biographies/New Age Pages 424 |
| ☐ | **Lip-Reading** by *Edward Nitchie* | ISBN: 1-59462-206-X | $25.95 |
| | *Edward B. Nitchie, founder of the New York School for the Hard of Hearing, now the Nitchie School of Lip-Reading, Inc, wrote "LIP-READING Principles and Practice". The development and perfecting of this meritorious work on lip-reading was an undertaking...* | | How-to Pages 400 |
| ☐ | **A Handbook of Suggestive Therapeutics, Applied Hypnotism, Psychic Science** by *Henry Munro* | ISBN: 1-59462-214-0 | $24.95 |
| | | | Health/New Age/Health/Self-help Pages 376 |
| ☐ | **A Doll's House: and Two Other Plays** by *Henrik Ibsen* | ISBN: 1-59462-112-8 | $19.95 |
| | *Henrik Ibsen created this classic when in revolutionary 1848 Rome. Introducing some striking concepts in playwriting for the realist genre, this play has been studied the world over.* | | Fiction/Classics/Plays 308 |
| ☐ | **The Light of Asia** by *sir Edwin Arnold* | ISBN: 1-59462-204-3 | $13.95 |
| | *In this poetic masterpiece, Edwin Arnold describes the life and teachings of Buddha. The man who was to become known as Buddha to the world was born as Prince Gautama of India but he rejected the worldly riches and abandoned the reigns of power when...* | | Religion/History/Biographies Pages 170 |
| ☐ | **The Complete Works of Guy de Maupassant** by *Guy de Maupassant* | ISBN: 1-59462-157-8 | $16.95 |
| | *"For days and days, nights and nights, I had dreamed of that first kiss which was to consecrate our engagement, and I knew not on what spot I should put my lips..."* | | Fiction/Classics Pages 240 |
| ☐ | **The Art of Cross-Examination** by *Francis L. Wellman* | ISBN: 1-59462-309-0 | $26.95 |
| | *Written by a renowned trial lawyer, Wellman imparts his experience and uses case studies to explain how to use psychology to extract desired information through questioning.* | | How-to/Science/Reference Pages 408 |
| ☐ | **Answered or Unanswered?** by *Louisa Vaughan* | ISBN: 1-59462-248-5 | $10.95 |
| | *Miracles of Faith in China* | | Religion Pages 112 |
| ☐ | **The Edinburgh Lectures on Mental Science (1909)** by *Thomas* | ISBN: 1-59462-008-3 | $11.95 |
| | *This book contains the substance of a course of lectures recently given by the writer in the Queen Street Hall, Edinburgh. Its purpose is to indicate the Natural Principles governing the relation between Mental Action and Material Conditions...* | | New Age/Psychology Pages 148 |
| ☐ | **Ayesha** by *H. Rider Haggard* | ISBN: 1-59462-301-5 | $24.95 |
| | *Verily and indeed it is the unexpected that happens! Probably if there was one person upon the earth from whom the Editor of this, and of a certain previous history, did not expect to hear again...* | | Classics Pages 380 |
| ☐ | **Ayala's Angel** by *Anthony Trollope* | ISBN: 1-59462-352-X | $29.95 |
| | *The two girls were both pretty, but Lucy who was twenty-one who supposed to be simple and comparatively unattractive, whereas Ayala was credited, as her Bombwhat romantic name might show, with poetic charm and a taste for romance. Ayala when her father died was nineteen...* | | Fiction Pages 484 |
| ☐ | **The American Commonwealth** by *James Bryce* | ISBN: 1-59462-286-8 | $34.45 |
| | *An interpretation of American democratic political theory. It examines political mechanics and society from the perspective of Scotsman James Bryce* | | Politics Pages 572 |
| ☐ | **Stories of the Pilgrims** by *Margaret P. Pumphrey* | ISBN: 1-59462-116-0 | $17.95 |
| | *This book explores pilgrims religious oppression in England as well as their escape to Holland and eventual crossing to America on the Mayflower, and their early days in New England...* | | History Pages 268 |

www.bookjungle.com *email: sales@bookjungle.com fax: 630-214-0564 mail: Book Jungle PO Box 2226 Champaign, IL 61825*

**QTY**

**The Fasting Cure** *by Sinclair Upton* — ISBN: *1-59462-222-1* **$13.95**
*In the Cosmopolitan Magazine for May, 1910, and in the Contemporary Review (London) for April, 1910, I published an article dealing with my experiences in fasting. I have written a great many magazine articles, but never one which attracted so much attention...* New Age/Self Help/Health Pages 164

**Hebrew Astrology** *by Sepharial* — ISBN: *1-59462-308-2* **$13.45**
*In these days of advanced thinking it is a matter of common observation that we have left many of the old landmarks behind and that we are now pressing forward to greater heights and to a wider horizon than that which represented the mind-content of our progenitors...* Astrology Pages 144

**Thought Vibration or The Law of Attraction in the Thought World** — ISBN: *1-59462-127-6* **$12.95**
*by William Walker Atkinson* — Psychology/Religion Pages 144

**Optimism** *by Helen Keller* — ISBN: *1-59462-108-X* **$15.95**
*Helen Keller was blind, deaf, and mute since 19 months old, yet famously learned how to overcome these handicaps, communicate with the world, and spread her lectures promoting optimism. An inspiring read for everyone...* Biographies/Inspirational Pages 84

**Sara Crewe** *by Frances Burnett* — ISBN: *1-59462-360-0* **$9.45**
*In the first place, Miss Minchin lived in London. Her home was a large, dull, tall one, in a large, dull square, where all the houses were alike, and all the sparrows were alike, and where all the door-knockers made the same heavy sound...* Childrens/Classic Pages 88

**The Autobiography of Benjamin Franklin** *by Benjamin Franklin* — ISBN: *1-59462-135-7* **$24.95**
*The Autobiography of Benjamin Franklin has probably been more extensively read than any other American historical work, and no other book of its kind has had such ups and downs of fortune. Franklin lived for many years in England, where he was agent...* Biographies/History Pages 332

| **Name** | |
|---|---|
| **Email** | |
| **Telephone** | |
| **Address** | |
| | |
| **City, State ZIP** | |

☐ Credit Card     ☐ Check / Money Order

| **Credit Card Number** | |
|---|---|
| **Expiration Date** | |
| **Signature** | |

*Please Mail to:* Book Jungle
PO Box 2226
Champaign, IL 61825
*or Fax to:* 630-214-0564

**ORDERING INFORMATION**

**web**: *www.bookjungle.com*
**email**: *sales@bookjungle.com*
**fax**: *630-214-0564*
**mail**: *Book Jungle PO Box 2226 Champaign, IL 61825*
**or PayPal** *to sales@bookjungle.com*

*Please contact us for bulk discounts*

**DIRECT-ORDER TERMS**

**20% Discount if You Order
Two or More Books**
Free Domestic Shipping!
Accepted: Master Card, Visa,
Discover, American Express

www.ingramcontent.com/pod-product-compliance
Lightning Source LLC
Chambersburg PA
CBHW081331040426
42453CB00013B/2374